Anji Burgan

SWINGING SEXTIES

GW00469251

AUSTIN MACAULEY PUBLISHERS™

LONDON • CAMBRIDGE • NEW YORK • SHARJAH

Chapter One
How It Began!

I had ended a three-year relationship with an ex-boyfriend. It was a good relationship, it had its ups and downs; like most normal relationships, I felt that it had become stale. I'd turned forty and suddenly felt like someone had removed my blinkers; I didn't like the life I witnessed before me. It was time to change and so I did; I stepped back into the lifestyle of being single. It felt strange to be single again, but I felt free and wanted to spend my time with my sons. Not interested in men or dating again, not straight away. Dedicating my time to work and meeting friends socially. I'd become mum again, enjoying my bond and relationships with my sons; they were the only male relationships I needed. One month passed and then another; by the third month I felt like I had my dating mojo back and decided it was time to enjoy and meet men socially for me. So I took the plunge and joined a well-known dating website suggested by a friend. Feeling excited creating the profile, uploading pictures, advertising myself to hopefully meet the man of my dreams.

I thought to myself, *what is the man of my dreams?* Smiling with a click of my fingers, my profile was complete and active. I sat for a while checking messages, nothing; so closing my profile I went about my day.

My day consisted of work and running around after my family until I finally arrived home. I opened my dating profile to see over forty new messages from potential dates within my inbox. My whole body quaked with excitement, I felt a pang of utter shock that men wanted to date me. Immediately responding to each message, I remained calm, not expecting anything to come from my pending dating experience. Some of these men were all-special in their own way, all wanting the same as me, to date and find their 'Miss Right!'

Conversion via messages with certain men and felt that I enjoyed finding out about them, their lives and what made them tick! I had a rush of excitement flowing throughout me; I loved to flirt, to tease and I realised then, I could do so by using words.

After weeks of conversing through messages online, I decided it was time to pluck the courage up and ask one man on a date, who had gained my attention with his looks, personality, and wittiness. His name was John, 6ft., athletic-build, brown hair, and a cheeky smile. We arranged to meet socially for coffee. Now anyone who's ever used a dating site before understands how frustrating it can be to fit a date in around each other's lifestyles. We eventually organised a coffee date that worked for us both at John's home. I questioned myself, "What are you doing, he could be a serial killer?" Doubting myself constantly I buried these feelings of anxiety under my belt. Driving over to John's house felt like an exciting blur. I pulled up outside his house, checked my appearance in my rear-view mirror; my nerves had kicked in leaving my body shaking. Climbing from my car I breathed the hugest breath I could and then made my way to his front door. Knocking on the door, shaking on the outside, excitement on the inside, my mind saying over and over "Don't be in, don't be in!" Before I knew it, the door swung open; a tall frame stood before me. I looked up and saw his smile; I quickly smiled back and then accepted his invitation inside his home.

Once inside his home I didn't pay that much attention to his homely comforts. My attentions were only towards John. He was lovely, very friendly and welcomed me into his home. My nerves were still surfacing, John could see how nervous I was, smiling while making coffee for us both, trying to relax me into the comfort of his presence and home. We sat chatting for a while talking about all kinds of topics, life, kids, dating and sex. I hadn't dated for a long time and certain topics had me blushing like a schoolgirl. John asked me "What's your fantasy? "I sat thinking for a few minutes; I knew what my dark fantasy was; could I, should I air it by voice? What would John think? Would he think I'm dirty, kinky, strange even?
Tilting my head, I sat glancing at him and then muttered a whisper, my voice small. "My fantasy is to be dominated by a suited man!"

I'd said it out loud. I felt a sense of relief but also a sense of guilt for revealing my hidden craved desire. Watching John's reaction to my fantasy, he didn't flinch an inch; he just smiled at me, moved closer towards me, close enough that I could feel his breath on my cheek, his stare looking down on me.

Softly he said, "Maybe I could help you out with your fantasy sometime?"

My whole body convulsed, I looked up at him with excitement dancing in my eyes, softly speaking words of amazement, "Ummm... I'd... Oh my god!"

Was this really happening? Is this man really a dominant man? The kind of dominant man I've always wanted to find. So many questions swirling around in my head. John smiled at me as if he could hear my thoughts; softly but firmly he pressed his lips over mine whispering, "That could be arranged!" Kissing him back I crashed against his athletic frame wondering if I'd found what I'd secretly been looking for.

After a cheeky kiss, I gently graced my hand in a sensual teasing rub and stroked over his bulging denim jeans, showing him there is more to come. We drank our strong coffee, sat closely together in a relaxing manner chatting a whole vocabulary of subjects. John mentioned a site for me to join; it's a lot like a dating site; meet for coffee, sex or exactly what I'm looking for. I had a look of sheer horror on my face; deep inside I had to check out this site. The name of the site was 'Swinging Sexties'.

I thanked John with a soft kiss for his time, coffee and then decided for another possible date. Climbing back into my car I drove home with one destination in my sight... to join this site of sex John had mentioned; to find out what it's all about!

CPSIA information can be obtained
at www.ICGtesting.com
Printed in the USA
LVHW080803120122
708213LV00016B/2425